The Wilder Nonprofit Field Guide To

Fundraising on the Internet

Gary B. Grant, Gary M. Grobman, and Steve Roller

AMHERST H.
WILDER
FOUNDATION

SAINT PAUL,
MINNESOTA

**We thank The David and Lucile Packard Foundation
and the Amherst H. Wilder Foundation for support of this publication.**

Published by the Amherst H. Wilder Foundation
Copyright © 1999 by Gary M. Grobman and Gary B. Grant

This work is excerpted and adapted from a larger work entitled *The Non-Profit Handbook* published by White Hat Communications, P.O. Box 5390, Harrisburg, Pennsylvania 17110-0390, phone 717-238-3787.

The Amherst H. Wilder Foundation is one of the largest and oldest endowed human services and community development organizations in America. For more than ninety years, the Wilder Foundation has been providing health and human services that help children and families grow strong, the elderly age with dignity, and the community grow in its ability to meet its own needs.

The Wilder Nonprofit Field Guide *series has been developed by the Wilder Publishing Center to help you and your organization find success with the daily challenges of nonprofit and community work. Other titles in this series include*

Conducting Successful Focus Groups
Developing Effective Teams
Getting Started on the Internet

More titles are in development—to see the latest, please visit our web site at WWW.WILDER.ORG. If you would like to submit an idea or manuscript to the series, please contact us at:

Publishing Center
Amherst H. Wilder Foundation
919 Lafond Avenue
Saint Paul, MN 55104
1-800-274-6024

Edited by Vincent Hyman

Manufactured in the United States of America

Second printing, May 2000

Library of Congress Catalog Card Number: 99-60083

ISBN 0-940069-18-0

Editor's note: The internet and world wide web are new, rapidly changing technologies. The information and web site addresses in this document may change during the life of this booklet. We apologize for any inconvenience this may cause.

 Printed on recycled paper
10% postconsumer waste

About the Authors

GARY B. GRANT received his bachelor of arts degree in history from the University of Chicago in 1987 and his Juris Doctor from Illinois Institute of Technology, Chicago-Kent College of Law in 1994. In law school, he served on the *Chicago-Kent Law Review* and the Kent Justice Foundation. He worked in the legal clinic providing legal advice to indigent civil defendants and served as an Everett Fellow with Citizens for Tax Justice in Washington, D.C. He has worked as a law clerk for the National Clearinghouse for Legal Services in Chicago, writing and editing articles for the *Clearinghouse Review*. Gary has also worked as a fundraiser for the University of Chicago and the University of Chicago School of Social Service Administration, where he currently is employed as associate dean for external affairs. He is a member of the National Society of Fundraising Executives and has served on the ethics committee of this organization, assisting in the publication *Honorable Matters, A Guide to Ethics and the Law in Fund Raising*. In his spare time, Gary serves as a vice president with the Hyde Park/Kenwood Community Conference, where he heads a project to build an internet gateway to the community and to promote use of the internet for nonprofit organizations and businesses. He teaches professional development classes on uses of the internet in social work.

GARY M. GROBMAN received his master of public administration degree from Harvard University's Kennedy School of Government and his bachelor of science degree from Drexel University's College of Science. He is in a Ph.D. program in public administration at Penn State University. Currently, he is the special projects director for White Hat Communications and the contributing editor for *Pennsylvania Nonprofit Report*. Prior to becoming a private consultant to government, nonprofit, and business organizations, he served for thirteen years as executive director of the Pennsylvania Jewish Coalition, a Harrisburg-based government affairs organization representing eleven Jewish federations and their agencies. He served almost five years in Washington, D.C., as a senior legislative assistant for two members of Congress and was a reporter and political humor columnist for the Capitol Hill independent newspaper *Roll Call.* In 1987, he founded the Non-Profit Advocacy Network (NPAN), which consists of more than fifty statewide associations representing Pennsylvania charities. He is the author of *Improving Quality and Performance in Your Non-Profit Organization; The Non-Profit Handbook, National Edition; The Pennsylvania Non-Profit Handbook;* and *The Holocaust—A Guide for Pennsylvania Teachers.* He is coauthor of *The Non-Profit Internet Handbook.*

STEVE ROLLER is manager of grant development with the Chicago Housing Authority, Grant Administration Department, where he is involved in identifying funding opportunities and preparing grant applications to support the creation, improvement, and expansion of programs and services for the Chicago Housing Authority's Office of Community Relations and Involvement. Prior to this, Steve was with the Chicago Housing Authority Department of Resident Management and Opportunities where he provided training and assistance to resident management organizations under the federal Tenant Opportunities Program. Steve has also worked as an assistant planner with the City of Chicago Department of Planning and Development and as a consultant with Chicago Youth Centers, a youth welfare agency. Steve received a master's degree in social administration from the University of Chicago, School of Social Service Administration.

Contents

Introduction
Should Fundraisers Be on the Net?

Chances are if you've bought this booklet, you know something about fundraising or something about the internet, but little about how both can be combined. Our goal is to help you see some specific ways you can use the internet to increase your expertise and success in fundraising. (If you know very little about the internet, please see another booklet from the Wilder Publishing Center, *The Wilder Nonprofit Field Guide to Getting Started on the Internet.* That booklet also contains definitions of many of the terms used in this one.)

The internet is an amazing new technology and tool. But can it be useful for fundraising? The answer is an unequivocal "yes"—the internet is an important tool for fundraisers. While no one would recommend that you base your fundraising strategy solely on the internet, it can save you time and money.

But where to start, and how can you use the internet? For the fundraiser, there are really two broad categories of use of the internet. With the internet, you can

1. Improve your *skills* as a fundraiser by using online magazines, networking with peers, and studying how others use the internet to raise funds.

Get Started Now!

You can learn more about fundraising on the internet—on the internet! See the online article *Fundraising and the Internet: Another Arrow in the Quiver* by Hewitt and Johnston Consultants (http://www.fundraising.com/intfundart.html). The authors of the article reason that charitable organizations should reach out to internet-using households, which have higher than average incomes and education and use the internet for both personal finance and shopping.

---

2. Improve your *fundraising success* by using the internet for prospect research, creating e-mail mailing lists and newsletters, cultivating donors, and offering opportunities for people to donate to your organization online.

This booklet is divided into two sections. Part I, Fundraising and the Internet, focuses on the many applications of the internet to the discipline of fundraising. In it, you will find tips for using the internet to learn more about the art of fundraising, using e-mail to attract and solicit support, prospect research on the internet, and building a web site to attract support for your organization. Part II, Web Sites of Note, contains reviews of a variety of web sites. We chose some of these sites because they are good examples for study. You may want to imitate some, or avoid problems you see in others.

So, you can use the internet to be a better fundraiser, to raise funds, and to study the competition. That said, let's get started!

Part I
Fundraising and the Internet

Increase Your Fundraising Skills

The internet got started in part as an information-sharing tool. While it now has many commercial or revenue-generating uses (including the use of the internet to raise funds), your first step in using the internet might be to learn more about fundraising by using three approaches that work well on the internet:

1. You can network with peers using various mailing lists.

2. You can find useful resources, such as creative fundraising ideas and books or courses on fundraising.

3. You can keep up with fundraising news by visiting the web sites for philanthropy publications.

One note of caution: If you have little experience as a fundraiser, don't rely solely on the internet to learn about fundraising. There is no guarantee about the accuracy of information online. Finally, be careful of any financial transactions on the internet.

Use the Net . . . to Network

If you really want to learn about fundraising, and you want to use the internet as a starting point, perhaps the best way would be to use it to access other professional fundraisers who may be willing to share and discuss issues pertaining to the field and to answer questions for newcomers. You may find colleagues on some Usenet newsgroups such as soc.org.nonprofits. Also, there are some mailing lists you could join, including the following:

- **CFRNET,** a list for people involved in corporate and foundation relations.

  To subscribe to this list send the text:
  subscribe cfrnet <your real name>
  in the body of the message to:
  cfrnet-request@medicine.wustl.edu

- **FUNDLIST,** a general mailing list for fundraising professionals.

  To subscribe to this list send the text:
  SUB FUNDLIST <your real name>
  in the body of the message to:
  listproc@listproc.hcf.jhu.edu

- **GIFT-PL,** a mailing list on planned giving.

  To subscribe to this list send the text:
  subscribe gift-pl <your real name>
  in the body of the message to:
  listserve@vm1.spcs.umn.edu

- **Fundraising Online**

  To get basic information about this list, send the text:
  info fundraising online
  in the body of the message to:
  majordomo@igc.org

That's just a start. More fundraising mailing lists can be found at

- **E-Mail Discussion Forums**
  (http://weber.u.washington.edu/~dlamb/apra/lists.htm)

Find Books, Courses, and Creative Fundraising Ideas

The second way to use the internet to improve your skills is to seek out helpful resources. There are a variety of search engines available to seek information. Chances are that if you enter the term "learn about fundraising" in any search engine, you will be more likely to find ads for books on fundraising (which might be helpful) and listings of seminars than to find volumes of detailed and comprehensive material on the subject. Books and courses on fundraising will likely be more reliable than information you find in internet documents. Books can also be found at online retailers such as www.amazon.com or www.barnesandnoble.com. If you visit these retail web sites and enter *fundraising*, *philanthropy*, or similar words in their site's search engine, you will uncover a number of books on a variety of special topics. (For more on using search engines, see our booklet *Getting Started on the Internet.*)

Depending on the kind of fundraising you do for your organization, you might be interested in exploring creative fundraising ideas: fun things to do, items to sell at a fundraiser, and the like. Besides getting ideas from others sharing their success stories, you might also search for companies that offer products for sale by charities. An example of one we found was Music Brokers for Charities (http://www.quiknet.com/dimple/used2.html). Your organization can collect used CDs and videos and Music Brokers will purchase them from you.

Visit Publications on Fundraising and Philanthropy

Fundraising is a time-consuming occupation. Time is in short supply for keeping up with news in philanthropy, the latest knowledge in the field, and participating in advocacy efforts related to current legislation and policies affecting fundraisers. The cost of subscribing to professional journals is not always a part of the fundraiser's budget and, if so, is often limited. The online solution is to visit relevant news sites or to subscribe to e-mail services providing such news in a way that is easier to search, convenient, and cost-effective.

Online articles and publications on philanthropy can enhance a fundraiser's ability by allowing for access to the largest number of information sources, usually free of charge. Keep in mind that you can't carry your computer on the bus for reading on the way to work, so we might recommend keeping your most important subscriptions arriving in hard copy through the mail. The internet, however, can be especially helpful for gathering information from sources that are either only available online, or that are secondary in importance to you. Even if you don't read your online sources for news regularly, it may be helpful on those occasions when you want to look through a variety of perspectives on a topic.

The following sites are among the online publications relating specifically to fundraising.

- **Philanthropy News Digest**
  http://fdncenter.org/phil/philmain.html

- **Philanthropy Journal Online**
  http://www.philanthropy-journal.org

- **Chronicle of Philanthropy**
  http://www.philanthropy.com

- **NonProfit Times Online**
  http://www.nptimes.com

Use the Internet to Help You Raise Funds

In addition to using the internet to improve your skills as a fundraiser, you can use it to help you raise funds. Specifically, you can

1. Conduct prospect research
2. Search for funding resources
3. Visit sites that assist donors
4. Use e-mail to attract and solicit support
5. Create a web site to attract and solicit support

Following are tips to help you with these tasks.

Conduct Prospect Research

Prospect research can take many different forms. Are you looking for information about an individual someone recommended to you as a possible supporter? Are you seeking to broaden your appeal to new individuals and corporations who have not yet been involved in your organization?

Below are some examples of the sites used by prospect researchers.

- **Internet Prospector**
  http://PLAINS.UWYO.EDU/~prospect

- **David Lamb's Prospect Research Page**
  http://weber.u.washington.edu/~dlamb/research.html

- **Hoover's Online**
  http://hoovweb.hoovers.com

- **Prospex Research**
  http://prospex.com/Welcome.html

- **CASE List of Prospect Research Sites**
  http://192.203.212.6/256/frprspct.htm

- **The Association of Prospect Researchers
  for Advancement**
  http://weber.u.washington.edu/~dlamb/apra/APRA.html

Using Automated E-Mail to Collect Development Opportunities

Gary Grant is a development officer at a school of social work. His interest in funding opportunities covers the gamut of topic areas, providing that the funding applies to research in areas of social work. Reviewing agency sites online periodically is impractical for him; however, several key agencies and organizations provide automated searches or reports as funding announcements are made. Gary receives the weekly National Institute of Health (NIH) guide via e-mail, as well as several other alerts. Skimming these for the ones applicable to social work research, he forwards them by e-mail to the faculty and doctoral students at his school. Most of what he receives could be obtained in printed form, but by using e-mail, he gets it into the hands of those who need it almost immediately, for less cost, and with less time spent in the effort than ever possible before.

Information like that provided at agency sites makes possible a level of searching and information-gathering never before possible. But to be realistic, only if you have a narrowly tailored interest area can you spend the time necessary to search each one. You may, therefore, want to find sites that either do the gathering for you and provide a comprehensive listing of opportunities, or enlist the assistance of a service that searches for you while you are off-line. Once you identify a possible funding opportunity online, the site describing the opportunity is likely to contain more helpful information necessary to you as you work through the application process.

Search for Funding Sources

Prospect research provides a tool to identify prospects and to collect relevant public information helpful to the fundraiser. Many funding organizations, however, use the internet to make information available to those who may want to apply for funding. The approaches you can use for finding funding sources online range from hunting to gathering.

Hunting for funding sources involves embarking on a search through the internet for support from a variety of sources at a single time when funding is needed. For example, if your organization is raising funds for a new program for survivors of domestic abuse, you would use a search engine to seek out organizations that might have an interest in your cause.

A *gathering* approach involves identifying particular funding sources and visiting them periodically (or otherwise collecting their information as it is updated) so that you can be first in line to learn of the availability of support.

There is no preferred method of finding funding. But if you can identify the sources that fit your profile, it is probably a better use of time to take a gathering approach and accumulate references to sites of value to you.

Many federal agencies have their own web sites and use them to post funding opportunities and detailed information on grant programs. A good place to visit is the Library of Congress's Internet Resource Page (http://lcweb.loc.gov/global/executive/fed.html). This list covers virtually the entire federal government, including the White House, all cabinet departments, and independent agencies.

Good places to start for finding funding sources are

- **The Foundation Center**
  http://fdncenter.org

- **The Internet Nonprofit Center**
  http://www.nonprofits.org

- **Putnam Barber's Page on Nonprofit Resources**
  http://www.eskimo.com/~pbarber

- **Goodwill Industries of America**
  http://www.goodwill.org

Fundraising on the Internet

There are many ways you can use the internet to help you raise funds. You can

1. Conduct prospect research

2. Search for funding resources

3. Visit sites that assist donors

4. Use e-mail to attract and solicit support

5. Create a web site to attract and solicit support

Trolling the Internet for Grants

Steve Roller works for the Chicago Housing Authority and is particularly interested in grant programs through the U.S. Department of Housing and Urban Development. Each month, Steve visits the HUD web site (http://www.hud.gov) and finds his way to the funding opportunities page (http://www.hud.gov/fundopp.html). Here, he reviews the current HUD Tentative NOFA (Notice of Funding Availability) Schedule (http://www.hud.gov/nofas.html) where he gets the earliest possible news of soon-to-be-announced programs. For example, seeing that the HUD Office of Community Planning and Development has already made available information on the Continuum of Care Homeless Assistance program, he downloads the complete document to his computer and prints it out the day it is released.

Other funding information on the HUD site includes details of programs by categories, including help for the homeless, youth programs, drug prevention programs, counseling services, research support, and more.

Similar information is available at sites for the U.S. Department of Education (http://www.ed.gov) through its Money Matters page (http://www.ed.gov/money.html), the U.S. Department of Health and Human Services (http://www.os.dhhs.gov) through both its Funding page (http://www.odphp.osophs.dhhs.gov/nonprofit/funding. htm) and its Partnership page (http://www.hhs.gov/partner), and other social service-related federal departments and agencies.

There are comparable resources available at the state level. For example, at the State of Illinois web site (http://www.state.il.us), you can click on "state agencies" to find a long list of links to various state departments, agencies, and offices. You may need to navigate around these sites a bit to determine if they have information posted on grants they award. If you don't see a heading for grants, or Requests for Proposals (RFPs), then look for such headings as "Programs," "Services," "Resources," or "About the Agency."

Visit Sites That Assist Donors

A number of web sites focus on attracting donors and providing them with information about charities and charitable giving. These donor resources are often helpful to fundraisers, especially those who want their organizations included among the charities to which donors might be referred.

While there may be success stories from ventures such as this, there is little hard data on just how successful they are. Such sites may represent the future of online philanthropy. The proliferation of web sites and the ease of disseminating false or misleading information could make it difficult for donors to know who to trust, so an online "consumer's" guide to philanthropies makes sense. Also, just as there are organizations dedicated to helping to disperse traditional charitable giving to worthy efforts, so, too, might there be a role for helping donors to navigate the overwhelming number of options available through the internet.

Another use for this type of site is to encourage and facilitate giving. Some of the sites referenced in this book, for example, are aimed at helping to simplify employer efforts to promote employee giving. In essence, they serve as online consultants for giving opportunities, either allocating funds to a variety of selected organizations or directing them to the donor's choice.

The National Charities Information Bureau (NCIB) (http://www.give.org) is an example of a site aimed at donors who wish to ensure that they are giving to charitable organizations that fit NCIB guidelines. Interested donors can order a free *Wise Giving Guide* and by signing on will receive news via e-mail of new information at the site. There is also a set of donor tips available at the site. An online reference guide can be used by donors to review whether any of four hundred organizations evaluated comply with NCIB standards. These standards are detailed at the site and relate to an organization's governance, purpose, and its programs. NCIB also evaluates information disclosed, methods of fundraising, reporting, budgeting, and the use of funds, among other criteria. The quick reference guide provides an easily scanned alphabetical list of organizations coded as to whether they adhere to the recommended standards, and whether information has not been disclosed by the organization. Every two weeks, a new charity is featured online with the results of its report published.

Another way to ensure the legitimacy of a charity is through the Council of Better Business Bureaus (CBBB) (http://www.bbb.org). The Philanthropic Advisory Service (PAS) at the site includes many, but not all, reports made by this organization relating to specific charities (inclusion is based on the frequency of requests). For example, a donor can click on the report for Mothers Against Drunk Driving and find whether it meets CBBB standards for charitable giving, when that evaluation was conducted, and when the evaluation will expire. If an organization does not meet one or more standards, the unmet standards are described so that donors can make the most informed choices possible.

Other information contained in these reports includes descriptions of an organization's programs, expenses, system of governance, and fundraising methods. CBBB forbids the use of its reports for fundraising or promotional purposes, but encourages donors to use them to become more educated from this objective source about the organizations they support. Reports not available online can be ordered. The site also includes Tips on Charitable Giving, Tips on Tax Deductions for Charitable Giving, and Tips on Handling Unwanted Direct Mail Appeals, among other useful information for donors.

International Service Agencies (ISA) (http://www.charity.org) is an effort to increase workplace giving by providing a single site to which donors can contribute if they are interested in supporting efforts to alleviate hunger, poverty, and the effects of war, oppression, and natural disasters. Donors can give to ISA or can designate gifts for particular organizations within ISA. ISA members are organized into categories of Children, Education, Hunger Relief, Medical Care, Refugees/Disaster Relief, and Job Creation/Economic Relief. Members do not need to have their own home page to participate, as ISA includes a descriptive page for each member.

A similar, related project, Relief Web (http://www.reliefweb.int) is organized by the United Nations Department of Humanitarian Affairs. Emergency areas around the world are monitored by the site, allowing individuals to focus on aid where it may be most needed at any particular time. The site also gives data on the amount of humanitarian assistance that has been provided each year from each nation. And it provides data on the humanitarian assistance provided in response to complex emergencies. Another humanitarian relief site is ReliefNet (http://www.reliefnet.org), which features an innovative "virtual relief concert" in support of humanitarian relief efforts.

Of course, the well-known centralized resource for donors seeking to contribute to a variety of efforts is the United Way (http://www.unitedway.org).

The Corporate Community Involvement Resource Centre (http://www.charitynet.org/CCInet/noframes/pages.html) provides a place to learn about corporate philanthropy efforts and provides corporations with a place to be recognized for their contributions to the community. For example, fundraisers interested in the Ben and Jerry's Foundation (http://www.benjerry.com/foundation/index.html) can find its site here and learn what projects have been funded, its mission and guidelines, and procedures for applying.

This site is a product of the United Kingdom's CHARITYnet (http://www.charitynet.org), which serves as another resource center for nonprofits and contributors. Some of the activities at this site include

- Add your organization or your corporate philanthropy site to its listing.
- Learn about the tax effects of giving.
- Use free internet space from CHARITYNet to build your own web site, which you can use for fundraising or other purposes.

Use E-Mail to Attract and Solicit Support

One often-discussed question is whether e-mail can be used for direct solicitations. According to Nielsen Media Research, more than 80 million people in the United States and Canada are online. We don't know how many of those have e-mail—but it's safe to assume that the numbers are large enough to warrant consideration of e-mail as a fundraising device.

While the internet is new, it appears that people who use the internet frown on soliciting people online. In general, there is a degree of fear among many e-mail users that they will soon be inundated with e-mail. Already, the presence of e-mail advertisements or "junk e-mail" (also referred to pejoratively as "spam") is raising fears and sending some internet users back to their more traditional ways of communicating. In addition, e-mail is an informal method of communicating, and solicitations should probably still be made in a more formal manner, such as a letter on your agency letterhead with an original authorized signature.

This could change. When the telephone first became popular, it was quite unclear what etiquette phone calls would demand. In fact, one very early practice was to send a letter to the person you wanted to call, announcing that you planned to call at a particular date and time, rather than surprising him or her with an unexpected call. It was not until much later, well into the 1970s, that phone solicitations began to be commonplace—at least those from institutions with which people were already involved, if not "cold calls" from organizations seeking new supporters. It is still common to precede phone solicitations with a letter informing your prospect base that you will be phoning to request their support.

E-mail solicitation is tempting on another level—reaching out to find new supporters. It offers an opportunity to solicit gifts from the largest possible audience in a way that is inexpensive and less time-consuming than either direct mail appeals or phone solicitations. As such, it may one day help to minimize the dollars spent finding new funders. But some of the same factors that make this a tempting opportunity also make it a dangerous risk. Step without caution on the wrong toes, and your organization could be the talk of the internet in all the wrong ways. Angry words about your organization's overzealousness could spread quite quickly and create problems far exceeding the advantages of the dollars you might raise.

One place to be especially cautious is on mailing lists and newsgroups. In both cases, participants defend the topical turf of their particular group with ardor. Even the most well-meaning appeals for action or support of ideological values not inherent in the subject that brings the group together may be attacked by flame messages. The reason for this is that most of these groups suffer from (or at least fear) being overwhelmed with irrelevant dialogue. To prevent this, they stamp out such tangential discussions immediately. Those who persist after a friendly, or not-so-friendly, warning risk the group moving to the next retaliatory step—spamming—in which hundreds of participants e-mail the wrongdoer, effectively flooding his or her mail box with angry messages. And if this still does not work, they may contact the offender's service provider and petition for his or her removal from the system.

So, unless you are participating in a group you know welcomes solicitations, you should refrain from this. As with any group, you should always read the discussions first, until you get a feel for what is proper and not proper in the group.

If you've used your e-mail for some time, you may have already noticed that commercial advertisers have started reaching out to lists of e-mail addresses they acquire. There are companies that compile e-mail address lists and provide others with the service of sending their message to them. Again, the benefits of this are unclear at best and the risk of being labeled for inappropriate behavior are too great for anyone to advise nonprofits to use these services.

But what about your existing constituency? Would they be put off by an e-mail solicitation? Even here, it's hard to tell for sure, but right now it is probably not advisable, except perhaps in the most special and extraordinary cases. A routine of doing this could lead people to request that they be taken off your list.

Should You Use E-Mail to Solicit Funds?

It's probably not smart to use e-mail to solicit donations. A much better use of e-mail is to simply interact with your constituency. Provide them with information and services that make them feel closer to your organization.

Perhaps a better use of e-mail is to simply interact with your constituency and to provide them with information and services that make them feel closer to your organization. E-mail can be a most convenient means for increasing the direct communication between you and your organization's actual and potential supporters. Sharing timely and informative news about what you are doing can keep you on donors' minds and make sure your work has visibility.

One way to do this is to organize a regular e-mail newsletter. Providing a consistent and dependable flow of information can allay fears of being overwhelmed by e-mail. As use of the internet and e-mail grows, this can help ensure that your e-mail lists grow, bringing a larger portion of your audience closer to your organization.

Another way is to develop a mailing list that you use to encourage dialogue among your organization's constituency. Some organizations, such as the Children's Defense Fund, provide an advocacy alert by e-mail and encourage their members to share information with others. This gives the organization the ability to almost instantly get word out to untold numbers of people, and in turn may bring many of these people closer to the organization.

Your constituency will enjoy the opportunity that e-mail gives them to provide input to your organization. Communicating, asking questions, and online surveys are some methods you can use to demonstrate how seriously you take such input. E-mail may also be used to inform people of events. This may be more successful than solicitations.

Finally, e-mail is used frequently to inform people of updates to a web site. This can help to bring people back when, although they find your site useful, they do not remember to return on a regular basis or know when to do so. A good way to increase your organization's constituency is by including a "guest book" at your site. Visitors "sign in," perhaps sharing what attracted them to your site. Visitors who sign an online guest book are probably more likely than the average person to stay involved over time. The web site administrator can collect guest book names and addresses and add them to the list of those who are kept up-to-date by e-mail.

In short, e-mail today is an outstanding tool for building a new kind of relationship with a broader base of participants in the life of your organization. It can help to develop a stronger bond without having to spend inordinate resources on events that bring people together. Building such relationships can only benefit your institution's short- and long-term fundraising prospects. Not only does it help to convey that your agency is doing important and exciting work, but it can help to make others feel as if they get something in return for their involvement by way of the close association e-mail communication allows.

Create a Web Site to Attract and Solicit Support

Increasingly, nonprofit agencies with web sites are including information or even special areas of their sites dedicated specifically to soliciting visitors for gifts. These range from noting the mailing address for donations to providing secure, online forms for making credit card contributions.

Sites asking for donations may

1. Explain how funds are used by the organization
2. Elaborate on the need for support and its impact
3. Describe donor options such as charitable gift annuities
4. Recognize current supporters or sponsors
5. Allow for inquiries about giving

The effectiveness of such sites is still to be determined. Some organizations, particularly larger ones, have reported substantial success raising funds through their web sites. Many people today are hesitant to donate online, however—either because of the perceived lack of security of the internet, or because of uncertainty about whether the nonprofit organization is legitimate. The larger agencies overcome the latter fears and may even offer secure pages for sharing credit card information.

A few examples of successful online web sites that solicit donations are

- **American Civil Liberties Union**
  http://www.aclu.org

- **American Cancer Society**
  http://www.cancer.org

- **American Red Cross**
  http://www.crossnet.org

- **Second Harvest**
  http://www.secondharvest.org

- **ALSAC/St. Jude Children's Hospital**
  http://www.stjude.org

- **Habitat for Humanity International**
  http://www.habitat.org

- **March of Dimes Birth Defects**
  http://www.modimes.org

- **Larry Jones International Ministries/Feed the Children**
  http://www.feedthechildren.org

Some common themes can be seen in these examples of fundraising sites. First, each makes it clear how support relates to, and advances, the mission of the organization. Each one directs visitors to online giving opportunities through various "how can I help" links. In the case of the American Cancer Society, support is appropriately solicited around the concept of providing a memorial to friends and loved ones lost to the disease that the organization battles. The ACLU focuses on attracting support to fight for freedoms relating to cyberspace, since so many visitors online are interested in this.

Second, many of them focus on attracting members, so that giving is not a one-time activity or a "one-way street," but rather establishes an ongoing relationship between the visitor-turned-donor and the organization. Visitors may be more likely to answer the call to become supporting members than simply to send a gift to an organization without establishing a formal relationship.

Third is the opportunity to provide donor recognition online. In the case of Project HOPE, the mere fact that it has a web site sponsor is an example of successful fundraising. Many commercial sites are funded through paid advertisements, so it's somewhat surprising that nonprofits are not taking more advantage of the publicity they can offer donors through their sites (especially if they provide something of value to a large audience). It is likely that the future will see more of this kind of funding arrangement and could help to reinvigorate corporate giving.

Fourth is the idea of providing donor education online. Providing some detailed explanation of such concepts as endowments, planned giving, and in-kind contributions is easy to do online, where the donor can control how much he or she reads. Doing this through printed media is more costly and risks overwhelming the potential supporter with too much information too early.

What Makes Online Fundraising Successful?

There are four elements common to most sites that seem to be having success raising funds online. These are

1. The site shows how a donation advances the mission and directs visitors to online giving opportunities.

2. The site focuses on attracting members and building an ongoing relationship between the organization and the visitor-turned-donor.

3. The site may offer donor recognition online, including opportunities to sponsor the web site itself.

4. The site includes pages that educate donors about giving, including concepts such as endowments, planned giving, and in-kind contributions.

How the Harry Singer Foundation Started Its Web Site

Margaret Bohannon-Kaplan and her husband, Melvin Kaplan, cofounded this national, private operating (not grantmaking) foundation with the goal of promoting responsibility and involving people more fully in public policy. Its stated goal is "to prepare individuals for a future where there will be less government and a weaker safety net."

"One of my husband's goals was to make the point that some people will invest time, effort, and money simply because they care—with no financial motives," says Kaplan, who serves as the Singer Foundation's director. "[Donors] pay for the opportunity to do some good."

Before creating a web site, the Singer Foundation offered a bulletin board service. Featured online were books using excerpts from the writings of high school students across the nation who responded to essay contests created by the Harry Singer Foundation. Kaplan says, "We also offered information relating to public policy as well as a Social Security Forum. But few people found our bulletin board, and [changes in] technology allowed us to consider going on the internet with a web site."

Among the most frustrating startup problems was finding a host web server, explains Kaplan. "We sent proposals to CompuServe, America OnLine (AOL), and Connect, a private web hosting service that catered to an exclusive clientele. Connect agreed to host our site but, unfortunately, it charged fees far in excess of those charged by AOL and CompuServe. This made it hard to attract our regular clients and Connect discouraged us from advertising our programs to their membership," she recalls. "Connect also restricted the site to ASCII and a small choice of icons."

But the beginning site nevertheless provided a good learning experience for the foundation. "Remember, this was before the arrival of the small internet service providers that can now be found in every part of the country," Kaplan adds. The site was maintained for a few years by part-time computer-literate students. Finally, in the spring of 1996, one of the foundation's volunteers started her own web design and webmaster business and donated time to develop the site further. In 1996, she wrote programs for submittal forms and added links to other sites.

"I submitted the material and direction, and the volunteer added HTML codes and made certain the material looked good on all browsers," says Kaplan. "But we took the entire job back to our office in May 1997. I am now serving as webmaster using Microsoft® FrontPage, which inserts the HTML codes automatically. We plan to add a powerful search engine to the site to enable students who entered essay contests in past years to browse the twelve published foundation books found in our Archive Forum and review online what they wrote as high school students."

The foundation is planning further improvements. "Our data show that the Emotional Intelligence Forum is very popular, and we intend to expand it and the Family and Responsibility Forums, which have a lot of interactive programs," Kaplan continues. "We also offer hundreds of books, audio tapes, and even a few video tapes to schools and other interested parties on our Resources Forum. But for the next couple of years, Another Way will be our main focus. We'll highlight grassroots activities in local communities and host those communities on this forum."

The project can be viewed at http://www. singerfoundation.org/main/way

Does it make sense for your organization to build a web site to raise funds? In general, good common sense and an understanding of cyberculture should be applied by any organization intending to build a fundraising site. Begin by asking some of the following questions:

1. Who is most likely to visit your organization's web site? Not every organization will find a ready online audience receptive to it. Organizations that deal with current topics in a rapidly changing environment, such as the American Civil Liberties Union, or that address global needs, such as Project HOPE, are more likely to find a responsive audience. Organizations that have a large potential constituency that is not easily identifiable, such as the American Cancer Society and the Rivers Network, are among those that can benefit from being online, because many people looking to become involved in personally important issues will seek them out on the world wide web.

   Agencies dealing with local or community issues may be less likely to benefit from a fundraising site, since their appeal is to a narrower audience that is perhaps less likely to use the internet to communicate with an organization located in the neighborhood.

2. If you are unsure that your agency can find a readily available audience online, can you offer content likely to attract people with potential to support your agency? Any organization that produces an online product, such as a service, newsletter with current information, or other helpful information, may enjoy a larger flow of traffic, especially if the site is properly marketed to search engines and directories and is maintained regularly. If visitors use your site in their work or other interests, they may feel sufficiently grateful— and perhaps impressed with the quality of your organization—to make donations.

   The strategy of depending on a "brilliant" idea to attract visitors carries a serious risk that the idea is already in use or will not be as valuable as you expected. More important, the material on your site should be related to your organization's mission. Using a commercial example, a telephone company providing health and fitness information is more likely to generate shrugs than they are links. On the other hand, a diaper company providing child care and child development information for parents may be more likely to succeed. (For example, see Pampers' Parenting Institute at http://www.pampers.com.)

Be cautious about the time commitment you invest in a site designed to seek potential funders. It is probably best to be certain that you are committed to what you offer online and then treat donations that your site attracts as a reward.

3. If you are committed to at least making it possible for donors to give online, consider how much of an effort is appropriate. Should you provide information on all forms of giving and address every possible method of making online gifts, or is it best to provide a simple request for donations? The answer here will depend on the extent to which you expect to attract funders. If you are building an organizational web site for other purposes, then adding the ability to give online may be simple enough to be worth doing, even if you expect only a handful of gifts.

4. Can you use your fundraising site to encourage traditional forms of giving? The idea of donor recognition online is becoming increasingly popular, even for organizations that do not otherwise solicit gifts online. Pictures of groundbreaking ceremonies, spotlights on donors, and other kinds of online donor recognition methods can enhance your stewardship programs while providing a good example to visitors. Should you include an entire honor roll of supporters online? This answer may depend on your constituency and whether or not they are likely to see it and appreciate it. The idea is worth considering, especially if your donors are particularly active on the internet.

As with e-mail, one of the best uses for a web site is simply to begin attracting prospective donors. Cultivation, online and through traditional means, can then be used to involve people in your organization and to develop their interests in the long term.

For more thoughts on using the internet in fundraising, see http://www.fundraisingonline.com.

This ends our exploration of how fundraisers can use the internet. In Part II of this booklet, we'll look at various web sites and what they have to offer.

Part II
Useful Sites for Fundraisers

Following are reviews of some sites especially useful to fundraisers. The list is by no means exhaustive. Use these as starting places for learning about fundraising on the internet and for studying how your colleagues are attracting constituents online. Please note that some of these sites will change during the life of this booklet.

The list is organized in the following categories:

Foundation-Related Sites

Regional Grantmaker Associations, Coalitions, and Networks

Associated Grantmakers of Massachusetts
http://www.agmconnect.org

Associated Grantmakers of Massachusetts was founded in 1970. Its mission is "to support and advance effective and responsible philanthropy throughout the Commonwealth." The home page has nine arrow links. Included on the site (by clicking on the Library Services button) is a series of seven tip sheets (click on Philanthropy 2000) providing technical information for those who wish to start a nonprofit in Massachusetts or find sources for grants. For example, there is a sample letter of inquiry one might send to a grantmaker. The Market Place button links to files concerning publications and other products for sale by the organization. There is a member list with links to their home pages where they exist, an events calendar, and a What's New This Week button that updates not only new additions to the web sites but new additions to the web sites of its members and counterpart organizations around the country. The Links button provides the web sites for regional media outlets, local academic centers with an interest in nonprofits, government links, links to grantmakers, local and national internet service providers, resource pages of interest to nonprofits, online e-journals, hundreds of Massachusetts nonprofit organizations, and regional grantmakers associations.

Coordinating Council for Foundations
http://www.hartnet.org/ccf

The Coordinating Council for Foundations is a membership association of Hartford-area grantmaking institutions, including public, private, and operating foundations, as well as corporate foundations and giving programs. The council's mission is to promote effective philanthropy. The site includes links to national nonprofit resources, information about its membership, publications, and a common application form. One useful file, Ways to Give, explains different ways to participate in philanthropy, from setting up one's own foundation to establishing a charitable remainder trust. There is a page set aside for news provided by members, but there was nothing there at the time of this review.

Council of Michigan Foundations
http://www.cmif.org

The Council of Michigan Foundations (CMF) is an association of more than 360 foundations and corporations that make grants for charitable purposes. It is a membership organization whose mission is to enhance, improve, and increase philanthropy in Michigan. Here you can find a Grantmaker's Kiosk with capsule summaries of current grants made to local groups, a compendium of grants that are in the online publication *Making a Difference: Grantmakers and Nonprofits Working Together* and *So You Want To Give*, an online publication encouraging charitable giving. Click on Library Services for a comprehensive, searchable database of articles and other materials on philanthropy.

Delaware Valley Grantmakers
http://www.libertynet.org/dvg

Delaware Valley Grantmakers is a regional (chiefly Pennsylvania, New Jersey, and Delaware) membership organization comprised of private, trustee-managed, corporate, and community foundations; charitable trusts; federated funds; and corporate giving programs. The site also includes a common grant application form and reporting form that are accepted by many of its members. The site includes a generous number of links to internet resources of interest to local and national nonprofits and a job bank.

Donor Forum of Chicago
http://www.uic.edu/~dbmaint/donors94.html

The site features the 1994 *Philanthropic Database* of the Metro Chicago Information Center and the UIC Academic Computer Center. This database is searchable by foundation, beneficiary type, grant purpose, support type, and recipient (there are more than three thousand recipients in the database). The site is a terrific place to start for identifying grantmaking foundations in your fields of interest, for researching your competitors for these grants, and for brainstorming about developing programs locally that may parallel pilot programs elsewhere. Click on Great Grants for summaries of grants submitted by members.

Searchable Web Sites

Some web sites have their own built-in search engine, which allows you to enter a keyword and search through the web site for appearances of that word. Such sites are called *searchable*. A built-in search engine is very useful for large sites that contain lots of information, and therefore can help encourage return visits to the site. Consider adding a search engine to your web site if you plan on offering many documents on a variety of topics.

Grantmakers of Western Pennsylvania
http://www.telerama.com/~gwp

According to its web site, "Grantmakers of Western Pennsylvania is an association of grantmaking organizations—foundations, corporations, and charitable trusts—of all sizes and purposes. Its mission is to improve the effectiveness of its members in the philanthropic community to meet the needs of the people, organizations, and communities of Western Pennsylvania." This simply constructed site includes a file on membership benefits, information about upcoming conferences and seminars, a calendar of events, links to its counterpart regional grantmaker associations, mission statement, links to its membership, a common grant application form used by its members, and the organization's values statement.

Indiana Donors Alliance
http://www.indonors.com

The Indiana Donors Alliance, a membership association serving Indiana's grantmaking community, "is dedicated to fostering responsible and creative philanthropy for the public good," according to its web site. "The Alliance acts as a catalyst for philanthropic action by providing information and education, by facilitating communication and collaboration, and by encouraging new opportunities for giving and volunteering." The site has lots of publications, documents, and files of general national interest, including newsletter articles from past issues that provide sound legal information, such as "Grantmaking to Organizations NOT Exempt Under Internal Revenue Code Section 501(c)(3)," and legal guidance on filing the annual 990 tax return. This is one of the better regional grantmaker sites to browse in search of new information.

The Indiana Donors Alliance site has a lot of publications of national interest.

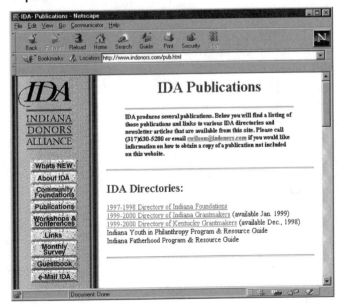

Used with permission.

Metropolitan Association for Philanthropy (St. Louis Area)
http://www.mapstl.org

The Metropolitan Association for Philanthropy is a regional association of grantmakers in metropolitan St. Louis, serving both donors and recipients to facilitate more effective philanthropy in the St. Louis region. The site has links to national and regional nonprofit and grantsmanship resources, information about its Foundation Center-sponsored library collection, and information about publications, many of which are available for free.

New York Regional Association of Grantmakers
http://www.nyrag.org

The New York Regional Association of Grantmakers is a nonprofit membership association of donors in the New York–New Jersey–Connecticut area. It promotes and supports effective philanthropy and concerted action for the public good. This is a colorful site, professionally designed and wonderfully constructed. It includes a file of local job openings in the philanthropic sector. When we reviewed this site, the calendar of events wasn't current, there were no general files of interest, and most of the documents related to internal aspects of the organization. One internal document we did find interesting was NYRAG's policy statement on diversity and inclusiveness, which could serve as a model for nonprofits in general who wrestle with this controversial issue. You can find this and other documents on the topic of diversity in philanthropy by clicking on Increasing and Diversifying.

Foundations

AT&T Foundation
http://www.att.com/foundation

The AT&T Foundation "is the principal instrument for AT&T philanthropy in the United States and throughout the world," according to the web site. The AT&T Foundation awards grants in the program areas of arts and culture, education, health and human services, international, and community services. Included is information about the foundation, the requirements for grant eligibility, and a file describing highlights of its grant program going back to 1984. Each of the program areas has a page that includes general information and links to some of the foundation's grantees. The site is animated and colorful, and includes a search-able database of grants made since 1994.

Ben and Jerry's Foundation
http://www.benjerry.com/foundation

The scoop about Ben and Jerry's Foundation is that it was established in 1985 and makes competitive grants to nonprofit organizations throughout the United States that facilitate progressive social change by addressing the underlying conditions of societal or environmental problems. Among the files you can access at this site are descriptions of grant recipients for each calendar quarter, foundation guidelines, foundation tips, and annual reports. To access the fun and creative home page of the parent corporation, click on the Site Index button.

The Ben and Jerry's web site "Fun Stuff" page.

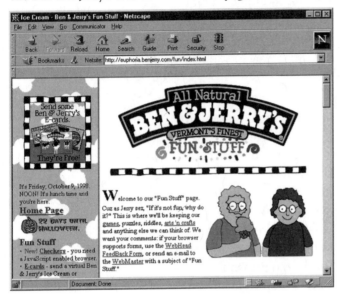

Used with permission.

Benton Foundation
http://www.benton.org

We found this to be one of the more attractive sites of a private foundation. Benton is a private foundation, based in Washington, D.C., that was founded in 1981 by Charles Benton, the son of U.S. Senator William Benton, who was the founder of Benton and Bowles and owner of the *Encyclopedia Britannica.* Its mission, according to the web site, is "to promote communications tools, applications, and policies in the public interest." This is a searchable, frame-supported, attractively designed site (as one would expect, since Charles Benton is the owner of a large communications company). There are links to pages of major programs of the foundation that have been set up with their own domain names, including the KidsCampaign, the Open Studio Arts Online, Destination Democracy (campaign finance reform), and Sound Partners for Community Health. Destination Democracy is an innovative advocacy site that uses the metaphor of a road map with road signs on how to achieve campaign finance reform. Sound Partners for Community Health is a collaboration of the Benton and Robert Wood Johnson Foundations and public radio stations. On this site, you can find a Benton "Toolkit" that includes a fascinating array of files relating to advocacy, online fundraising, and developing a web page.

Carnegie Corporation of New York
http://www.carnegie.org

Carnegie Corporation of New York was created by Andrew Carnegie in 1911 to promote the advancement and diffusion of knowledge and understanding. The corporation's capital fund, originally donated at a value of about $135 million, had a market value of $1.37 billion on December 31, 1996. The web site includes files of recent grants, publications, press releases, and links. There are files on Carnegie's special initiatives, including the Carnegie Commission on Preventing Deadly Conflict, the Carnegie Task Force on Learning in the Primary Grades, and the Carnegie Task Force on Meeting the Needs of Young Children. The site also has a file on grant restrictions, and instructions on how to submit a proposal to the organization.

Global Fund for Women
http://www.igc.apc.org/gfw

"The Global Fund for Women is an international organization which focuses on female human rights. It supports issues as diverse as literacy, domestic violence, economic autonomy, and the international trafficking of women, among others," according to its web site. Click on Your Help to make a pledge, and add your name to the organization's mailing list. You can find an online grant request form for grants, which range from $500 to $15,000.

Robert Wood Johnson Foundation
http://www.rwjf.org

The Robert Wood Johnson Foundation, based in Princeton, New Jersey, is the nation's largest philanthropy devoted exclusively to health and health care. The searchable site includes publications (click on Library) explaining the guidelines for applying for grants, annual reports, information about data collections, the foundation's newsletter, information about its current programs, and nearly a dozen publications, reports, and studies. Click on Last Acts for a file relating to the foundation's program on the issue of end-of-life health care.

George Lucas Education Foundation
http://glef.org

Established in 1991 by the famous filmmaker, this foundation does not provide grants or scholarships but promotes education, especially those activities that integrate technology with teaching and learning. The site includes sound files and movie files that would be of interest to educational institutions. Also on the site is the e-journal *Edutopia,* with current and back issues. At the time of our review, the latest issue had full-text articles on assistive technology and other education-related issues for people with disabilities. Although the foundation does not offer grants, it has links to government, foundation, and corporate sites that do. Also included are links to sites with general information about grants.

John D. and Catherine T. MacArthur Foundation
http://www.macfdn.org

The John D. and Catherine T. MacArthur Foundation is a private, independent grantmaking institution dedicated to helping groups and individuals to improve the human condition. The Hot Links button brings up hundreds of organizations and institutions who are current or former recipients of foundation grants. It provides links to those organizations that have web sites. This searchable site includes links to related organizations and nonprofit resources, grant information resources, and information about the foundation's programs.

Mitsubishi Electric America Foundation
http://www.meaf.org

The mission of the Mitsubishi Electric America Foundation (MEA) is "to contribute to the greater good of society by assisting young Americans with disabilities, through education and other means, to lead fuller and more productive lives," according to the web site. The site has an online guidelines brochure explaining how to apply for a grant, and files with information about current grant recipients with summaries of the projects being funded. The foundation also operates the Starfish Enterprise Award, presented annually to an MEA employee for the best volunteer project. A useful publication available on this site is *Road Map—*

Sustaining Project Impact: Guidelines for Evaluation and Dissemination. It is a full-text, comprehensive primer on outcomes evaluation and dissemination written by two Ph.D.s. There is information available on how to obtain a free hard copy of the publication, which is one of the most useful documents for non-profits we have seen on the web.

The David and Lucile Packard Foundation
http://www.packfound.org

The David and Lucile Packard Foundation was created in 1964 by David Packard, cofounder of the Hewlett-Packard Company, and his wife, Lucile. Grant recipients are principally universities, national institutions, community groups, youth agencies, family planning centers, and hospitals. The site includes guidelines for qualifying for a grant, the procedures for making an application, the foundation's annual report, and information about foundation programs and priorities. The site also includes a link to the electronic version of the free publication *The Future of Children*, published three times a year by the Foundation. The full text can be downloaded using Adobe® Acrobat® Reader available free at this site.

Pew Charitable Trusts
http://www.pewtrusts.com

The Pew Charitable Trusts, based in Philadelphia, is a national philanthropy established forty-nine years ago that seeks to "encourage individual development and personal achievement, cross-disciplinary problem solving and innovative, practical approaches to meeting the changing needs of a global community," according to its web site. Each year, the Pew Charitable Trusts make grants of about $180 million to between 400 and 500 non-profit organizations. This searchable site includes guidelines for obtaining a grant and the procedures to submit an application, information about recent grants and programs, and organizational press releases.

The Packard Foundation site includes its grant guidelines and other publications, all of which can be downloaded or ordered in hard copy.

Used with permission.

Rockefeller Brothers Fund
http://www.rbf.org

The Rockefeller Brothers Fund is a private, philanthropic foundation created in 1940. At the end of 1997, the foundation's assets were $454 million. The fund's major objective is "to improve the well-being of all people through support of efforts in the United States and abroad that contribute ideas, develop leaders, and encourage institutions in the transition to global interdependence." One of the program interests is to promote and sustain a vital nonprofit sector, both nationally and internationally. Files on this searchable site include information about grants awarded by the foundation, grant application procedures, publications (such as the annual report, grant guidelines, and papers/reports), and foundation programs. Click on the Links area for a generous supply of links to general nonprofit and foundation sites related to sustainable resources and South Africa. Click on the photo labeled "nonprofit sector" for information about grants targeted to sustaining a healthy voluntary sector.

The Rockefeller Brothers Fund site.

Used with permission.

Harry Singer Foundation
(See page 18 for more information.)
http://www.singerfoundation.org

The foundation was founded in 1987 for the purpose of promoting an increase in public involvement in public policy. The site provides information about donating public policy books to institutions, about its essay contests, and about its social studies workbooks.

Surdna Foundation
http://www.igc.apc.org/surdna

Surdna Foundation Inc. was established in 1917 by John E. Andrus, a businessman and investor who served as mayor of Yonkers, New York, and as a member of Congress. Surdna's grantmaking activities are concentrated in four programmatic areas: environment, community revitalization, effective citizenry, and the arts. Included on the page is a file discussing guidelines

How Rockefeller Brothers Fund Built Its Web Site

According to Karin Skaggs, communications assistant for the New York City–based Rockefeller Brothers Fund, the web site (http://www.rbf.org) was developed by Jennifer Hortin, a systems administrator no longer with the fund, about six months after the foundation determined that establishing a world wide web site was both technologically and economically feasible, and that it was an appropriate way to reach its intended audience more efficiently and with more timely information.

Formatting and coding were done in-house; graphics were designed by an outside source. Set-up costs were $800 for the Rockefeller Brothers Fund pages, which receive about 400 hits each week, and $2,250 for a related site called Project on World Security. That site went online in 1997.

Both sites are updated in-house, and a major graphic redesign of the RBF main site was in the works when we talked to Skaggs. She says that while the web site has increased the public's exposure to the fund's mission and programs, the number of inquiries received from prospective grantseekers has increased dramatically. In addition, because communication between grantseeker and foundation is as easy as a click of the mouse, some grantseekers do not focus as carefully on the RBF's specific grant guidelines. When the site was first established, staff members were not sufficiently prepared to deal with the increase in inquiries, but they now feel they have an effective response system in place.

The site's target audiences are grantees, grant seekers, and, on the linked site for the Project on World Security (www.rbf.org/rbf/pws), researchers and experts in the security field. Skaggs credits the web site with a significant increase in the number of inquiries received from prospective grantseekers.

"Once we develop our new site, it will become much easier for us to send publications and requests for information to people in electronic form, including eventually putting our annual report online," she says. "Certain foundations are considering an electronic version of their reports over and above the printed version. We would like to encourage even more communication among grantees; we will work toward this goal on our revamped site."

Skaggs believes the internet has made a positive contribution to improving communication between foundations and grantees, as well as between foundations and the public.

"In general, grant-giving organizations are finding the internet to be an effective tool for reaching grantseekers and grantees," asserts Skaggs. "It also appears that grantseeking organizations are taking advantage of the internet to seek funding sources and volunteers. In both cases, the internet provides an opportunity for organizations to communicate substantive information about their mission and work."

for applying for grants and restrictions concerning them. The foundation does not generally fund individuals, capital campaigns, or building construction. A description of this foundation's approach to grantmaking, general information about the foundation (including its trustees, officers, and staff), grantmaking program areas of interest, and guidelines for applying for funding can be accessed from links at the home page.

The "Essay Contest" page from the Harry Singer Foundation site.

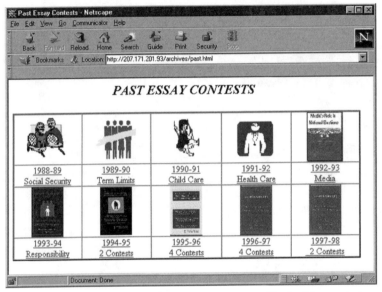

Used with permission.

Charity Sites

Top Forty Charities

How are mainstream charities using the internet to promote their organizations? The following are capsule reviews of the web sites of the top forty charities (using 1995 data), as ranked by the Internet Nonprofit Center. Use these summaries to identify sites where you can obtain useful information and get ideas for designing your own site. (The sites are listed in alphabetical order, not according to the size of the charity.)

ALSAC/St. Jude Children's Hospital
http://www.stjude.org

Memphis's St. Jude Children's Research Hospital focuses on the research and treatment of catastrophic diseases in children, primarily pediatric cancers. Its web site is searchable and in-

cludes a virtual museum giving the history of the facility. It has a
secure order form (click on How You Can Help) to make donations,
scores of useful links to related private and government organizations, plenty of files providing general health information, and a
plethora of frequently updated information in a pleasing, acces-
sible format—all of which encourages people who are interested in
medical research to return to the page again and again. This is a
good place to start for simple explanations of scores of major
diseases.

American Cancer Society
http://www.cancer.org

This searchable, frame-supported site has a host of information on
cancer, as well as other information pertaining to local and national American Cancer Society activities. There is wonderful
material promoting the "Great American Smokeout" day, which is
a model for communicating information about a special program
or event. Visitors can make an online contribution using a secure
form. Obviously, this is the place to start for information on what
is perhaps America's most dreaded disease.

American Heart Association
http://www.amhrt.org

Included on this searchable web site is a button that links to
AHA's database of news media releases and advisories with
Reuters Health Information Services. Visitors can make online
donations. A new feature permits the sending of free Heart-to-
Heart e-cards suitable for birthdays and other occasions, which
also promote the organization by delivering a message about heart
disease and a link to the web site. Recipients of the card receive
an acknowledgment of any donation you make to the organization
in their honor—a great fundraising idea. AHA's web site is *the* site
for information about cardiovascular disease, prevention, and
clinical cardiology.

American Lung Association
http://www.lungusa.org

The American Lung Association is the largest organization in this
country fighting lung disease, including asthma, emphysema, and
lung cancer. Information can be found on the site about making
donations and the tax advantages of doing so. You can donate
online on secure forms. The home page has a cute animation of a

pair of lungs in the process of breathing. The pages are searchable (the term "asthma" turned up matches in hundreds of files) and include information about important legislation pending on Capitol Hill, articles from associated medical journals that are re-edited to make them more understandable to the public, an A to Z encyclopedia of lung diseases, and association press releases. We *breathed easier* when we discovered that all of this information was available for free with just the click of a mouse!

The American Red Cross home page.

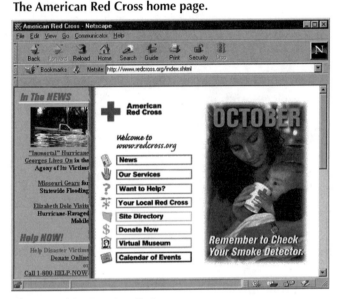

Courtesy of the American Red Cross. All Rights Reserved in all Countries. Visit the American Red Cross at www.redcross.org.

American Red Cross
http://www.redcross.org

This searchable site has the latest news concerning natural disasters and general/world news relating to natural and man-made disasters. Included in the site is a virtual museum giving the history of the agency. The colorful graphics, world-class design, and good information make it worthy of return visits. There is plenty of information concerning how to donate to the organization, including forms to make secure credit card transactions. This site sets the standard for charitable organization web sites.

AmeriCares Foundation
http://www.americares.org

AmeriCares is a private, international nonprofit disaster relief and humanitarian aid organization. The pages are simple and detail the disaster relief organization's efforts here and overseas. Click on Home Front for a file describing AmeriCares' program to do a one-day community-based home repair blitz for those with physical or financial limitations.

Big Brothers Big Sisters of America
http://www.bbbsa.org

This web site says the mission of Big Brothers Big Sisters of America "is to make a positive difference in the lives of children and youth, primarily through a professionally supported one-to-one relationship with a caring adult, and to assist them in achieving their highest potential as they grow to become confident, competent, and caring individuals, by providing committed volunteers, national leadership and standards of excellence." This frame-supported site (with text version) is simple and functional in design, with information about the organization, press releases, studies about the effectiveness of the organization's programs, an online donation form, information about volunteering with links to state organization affiliates, and links to local agencies. The site has a file on the community benefits and cost-effectiveness of its programs.

Boys and Girls Clubs of America
http://www.bgca.org

"The Boys and Girls Club Movement is a nationwide affiliation of local, autonomous organizations and Boys and Girls Clubs of America working to help youth of all backgrounds, with special concern for those from disadvantaged circumstances, develop the qualities needed to become responsible citizens and leaders," according to the web site mission statement. This frame-supported site includes video and audio clips of Denzel Washington speaking on behalf of the organization and a YouthWeb area of web sites that have been built by Boys and Girls Clubs. There are pages devoted to the organization's programs, an entire page lauding the corporate sponsors of BGCA, and lots of interestingly designed pages. Click on the Power of People and Alumni Hall of Fame for a list of well-known alumni.

Boy Scouts of America
http://www.bsa.scouting.org

This site is geared more toward encouraging scouting and activities for youth, rather than toward promoting the organization itself, seeking donations and volunteers, and the usual mission statements and annual reports. The BSA deserves a merit badge for its recently upgraded site design, which is searchable and frame-supported. It lets you scout around for information on the organization's new Venturing Program, its 19th World Jamboree, and instructions for starting a new scout unit. The site promotes BSA's magazines and official gear. This is a good site to study how a nonprofit organization promotes its products.

Campus Crusade for Christ
http://www.ccci.org

Campus Crusade for Christ is "an interdenominational ministry committed to helping take the gospel of Jesus Christ to all

Nations," according to the site. This is a searchable web site, available in six languages (English, Spanish, Russian, Czech, Slovenian, and Tagalog). You can download and listen to RealAudio files, or the entire two-hour film *Jesus.* There is not much in the way of appeals for donations on this searchable site. Click on What If for short, inspirational stories promoting the religious values of the organization.

Catholic Charities USA
http://www.catholiccharitiesusa.org

Catholic Charities USA is the largest private network of social service organizations in the United States. The section relating to Capitol Hill testimony and news releases is a good source for those interested in material relating to social services advocacy. New material has been added to promote its new adoption search manual for professionals and how to celebrate National Care Givers Week. Click on News Media and Our Opinion for speeches and remarks by organization officials at various conferences and press conferences.

Catholic Relief Services
http://www.catholicrelief.org

Catholic Relief Services was founded in 1943 by the Catholic Bishops of the United States. "In over 80 countries throughout Africa, Asia, Europe and Latin America, Catholic Relief Services (CRS) serves the poor by providing emergency and long-term assistance based on need, not creed, race, or nationality," according to the web site. The web site provides further information about the mission of the organization, how to contribute, and the history of the organization. Bulletins on recent national disasters and the organization's response to them can be accessed from the home page. You can donate by using a secure form and designate your gift to the annual fund or the disaster response fund.

Christian Broadcasting Network
http://www.cbn.org

CBN's mission is "to prepare the United States of America, the nations of the Middle East, the Far East, South America and other nations of the world for the coming of Jesus Christ and the establishment of the kingdom of God on earth." And perhaps in cyberspace as well. This colorful site is in an e-magazine format that is updated daily. It has an online pledge form, links to organizations that share CBN's values, and information about its programs. There are online Bible tracts and scripture references for counselors dealing with common problems. The site has plenty of professionally designed information about the network's founder, Pat Robertson, and his 700 Club.

Christian Children's Fund
http://christianchildrensfund.org

The Christian Children's Fund is one of the largest independent child care and development organizations. The frame-based site includes frequently asked questions, information on donations and how to sponsor children, updates on natural disasters, press releases (click on Christian Children's Fund News), and links to related organizations and to local affiliates.

Focus on the Family (James Dobson)
http://www.family.org

"Dedicated to the preservation of the home," according to the site, the Focus on the Family web pages include views on current events from the organization's leader, Dr. James Dobson. It is updated daily and also promotes publications by Dobson, explains where to hear broadcasts by the organization, and has an online donation form. Click on Parent's Place for inspirational advice on parenting, illustrated with references to the New Testament. The Hot Issues button links to the organization's CitizenLink, which, when we visited it, had an article on abstinence education that some may find easy to digest and others may find hard to swallow.

Gifts-In-Kind International
http://www.giftsinkind.org

Gifts In Kind International, according to the web site, is "the leading charity in the field of product philanthropy, helping companies donate product efficiently and effectively to charities and schools in your home town and around the world." This frame-supported site includes files on the benefits of making donations, how to qualify for receiving donations, a list of local coordinating agencies that process donation requests (typically local United Ways), and an online donation request application form. The site is simple and well-organized, getting you where you want to be without unnecessary trouble. Click on Year 2000 for Y2K resources and links to government, legal, private sector, and technical sites, one of the best gateways on the web for resources on this vexing issue of importance to nonprofit organizations.

Girl Scouts of the U.S.A.
http://www.gsusa.org

The Girl Scouts is the largest voluntary organization in the world for girls. Information is available at this site about affiliates, Girl Scout cookies, publications, awards, history of the organization, information about making donations, and how to become one of the 800,000 Girl Scout volunteers. The site includes an animated shopping mall and catalog section to market books, sports and camping equipment, and uniforms using a secure form. There are links to local affiliates that have web pages of their own.

Goodwill Industries
http://www.goodwill.org

Goodwill Industries is one of the largest providers of employment and training services for people with disabilities and barriers to employment. The colorful, animated, and searchable site links to its local affiliates, nonprofit information sources, other charities, government offices, organizations and offices related to disabilities, and computer and internet technical assistance and information. Click on Real People, Real Jobs for features on Goodwill, Graduates of the Year and Achiever of the Year.

Habitat for Humanity International
http://www.habitat.org

Habitat for Humanity International is a nonprofit, ecumenical Christian housing ministry dedicated to eliminating substandard housing and homelessness. It is best known for former President Jimmy Carter's active participation. The organization has an online catalog, but orders are taken through an 800 number rather than online. There is a section of organization press releases, and a searchable database of organizational affiliates. This site also solicits donations and provides information about volunteer opportunities. It is a pleasant, functional site, with additional versions in Spanish, French, and Norwegian.

Institute of International Education
http://www.iie.org

The Institute of International Education provides programs and services to promote international cooperation on business, diplomacy, the environment, hunger, and arms control. It conducts statistical and policy research and provides information on international study. This searchable site has a simple, colorful, inviting design. There is not a lot of substance other than information about programs, membership, board, mission, and programs, and other internal organizational matters. You can search listings of more than 4,000 academic year or short-term study abroad programs and obtain information about many of the 240 different international education programs administered by the organization, although some of the databases are restricted to members only.

International Planned Parenthood Federation
http://www.ippf.org

International Planned Parenthood's entire strategic plan is on the internet.

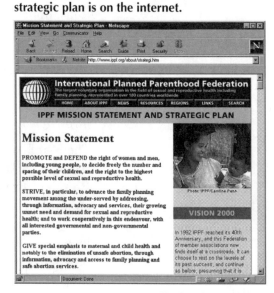

Used with permission.

International Planned Parenthood Federation is the largest voluntary organization in the world concerned with family planning and sexual and reproductive health. Included on the site is a file called "The Need for Family Planning," which explains the activities of the organization; information about making contributions, and what each contribution amount can purchase; links to its affiliates and related international and national government and private related organizations; and information about the organization's publications. Also included are organizational governing documents and the organization's strategic plan. This is one of the few national charities that posts its entire strategic plan on the internet. (Click on About IPPF and Mission Statement and Strategic Plan—Vision 2000.) This document is useful to those organizations thinking about creating their own web site.

Larry Jones International Ministries/Feed the Children
http://www.feedthechildren.org

Feed the Children is an international, nonprofit Christian relief organization. It has a nicely designed web site, with information about donations prominent, including a secure online form. It is colorful and inviting. There are pictures of hungry kids beckoning you to contribute and an electronic newsletter, *Frontline Report*, with information about sponsoring children. It proudly informs visitors that the site is built and maintained strictly inhouse without the use of outside consultants.

MAP International
http://www.map.org

MAP International is a nonprofit Christian relief and development organization. Included at the site is the online Resource Center, which serves as a developing library of internet resources on selected world health topics. These include updates on the most urgent humanitarian and disease emergencies around the globe, including links to internet sites that track the emergencies; global health reports; country and regional information; and a listing of e-mail discussion lists on international health topics, with instructions about how to subscribe and unsubscribe. The Get Involved button leads to a form that lets the organization send you publications, financial information, and information about contributions, volunteering, and how to participate in the organization's projects and programs. Click on The Pulse for a promotional message that is a teaser with a link to the Get Involved file.

March of Dimes Birth Defects
http://www.modimes.org

The March of Dimes is a nonprofit organization dedicated to reducing birth defects and infant mortality. Established in 1938 by President Franklin Delano Roosevelt to put an end to polio, the organization accomplished this mission within twenty years with Dr. Jonas Salk's development of the polio vaccine. The web site includes information on March of Dimes history, news items, pregnancy and childbirth, teen pregnancy, birth defects, local chapters, and volunteering. This is an excellent site for information about birth defects. An online form is provided for making donations via credit card. The site has files related to fundraising, donations, and volunteering to raise money. The site is searchable and has a wealth of information in both English and Spanish versions.

Metropolitan Museum of Art
http://www.metmuseum.org

The Metropolitan Museum of Art in New York City is one of the largest and best-known art museums in the world. This site is designed to give visitors an overview of the collections on display in the museum's galleries. Also on this site is a floor plan; information on services for visitors; a calendar offering a detailed current listing of special exhibitions, concerts, lectures, films, and other museum activities; and a gift and book shop, with more than one hundred of the institution's best-selling items for sale. This site is simply wonderful and can serve as the model for museums. There is membership information, online encryption for purchasing from museum shops, a generous taste of the exhibits, news about the museum, detailed information about most of the museum's holdings, and an innovative educational section for children, adults, and teachers. There are files that tell you everything you would want to know about the facility. Visiting this site will not replace visiting the place in reality, but museums should look at this site for hints on how to do an effective web site that will encourage return visits. A tasteful Sponsor's Page provides even more museum content, each with unobtrusive links to the home pages of the corporate sponsors of each highlighted exhibit.

You can click on a section of the museum's floor plan to get details about that section.

© The Metropolitan Museum of Art
Used with permission.

Muscular Dystrophy Association
http://www.mdausa.org

The Muscular Dystrophy Association (MDA) "is the definitive source for news and information about forty neuromuscular diseases, MDA research and services available to adults and children with neuromuscular diseases and their families," according to its web site. The site features viewable segments from Jerry Lewis's Labor Day weekend telethon and a secure online pledge form, information about volunteering, and information on how to make donations of durable medical equipment. There is a link to an online "ask the experts" bulletin board run by the organization and a searchable database of 230 MDA clinics. There are links to current and back issues of MDA's bimonthly *Quest Magazine*, with colorful graphics and full-text content, and the ALS newsletter.

National Association for the Exchange of Industrial Resources
http://www.freegoods.com

The Illinois-based National Association for the Exchange of Industrial Resources is "a nonprofit organization that collects and processes donations of new, top quality merchandise from American corporations, then redistributes those goods to qualified schools and nonprofits across the United States," according to information on the web site. The home page links to two files—how 501(c)(3)s can join the organization and receive benefits and how companies can make tax-deductible donations. The organization issues catalogs every ten weeks. Charities order from them (and average about $2,000 worth of supplies) and pay shipping and handling costs in addition to a fee for each

This is the page telling how to join NAEIR and what items are available.

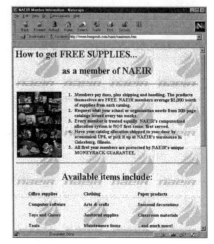

Used with permission.

catalog, which averages about $115 each. The site has forms to request information packets for both prospective donors and recipients.

National Easter Seal Society
http://www.seals.com

Founded in 1919, Easter Seals is a nationwide network of 109 affiliate societies operating programs to serve the disabled and their families. There are links to Housing, History, What's New, Legislation and Policy, Annual Report, and other pages. Here you can find information about the Society's Friends Who Care program (helping school children empathize with those with disabilities), information about donating and volunteering, and information about Project Action, a congressionally created national technical assistance program to improve access to transportation for people with disabilities.

The Nature Conservancy's site includes interactive stories from the latest *Nature Conservancy* magazine.

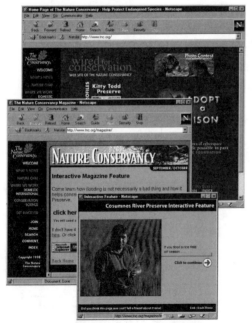

Used with permission.

The Nature Conservancy
http://www.tnc.org

The Nature Conservancy is an international environmental organization that seeks to preserve nature by purchasing and preserving endangered habitats. This colorful, professionally designed site is worth visiting, provided your browser supports frames and you have a fast modem. The site is searchable and has more than twenty audio and video clips and more than three hundred nature photos. Click on What's News and see an interactive feature story from the latest *Nature Conservancy* magazine. Each Wednesday, a trivia quiz is posted, and the winner receives Conservancy merchandise— a creative gimmick to encourage return visitors. Fill out an online survey and receive a free Conservancy screen saver. There is regularly changing content that is archived and an index of past *Nature Conservancy* issues. You can sign up or renew membership, volunteer, purchase merchandise, contribute money or materials, and even adopt a bison or an acre of rain forest. A secure credit card order form is provided online. This site also features a free e-card program. The Nature Conservancy web site is state-of-the-art, fun to browse, and designed to keep people coming back for more.

Project HOPE/People to People Health
http://www.projhope.org

Project HOPE (Health Opportunities for People Everywhere), established in 1958, is an international health education foundation providing health policy research and analysis, training for health care professionals, and consultations in health systems planning and development. HOPE was originally known for the S.S. *HOPE,* the world's first peacetime hospital ship, which had its maiden voyage in 1960. The site is searchable, and there is a form for making donations online, including credit card donations. Web surfers can go to a "quick jump" feature where they can scroll through the locales that have Project HOPE programs or projects and launch a page about what is happening there—just click on Project HOPE's international health education program from the home page. Included is a link to the Project HOPE Center for Health Affairs (CHA), founded in 1981, a nonprofit health policy research organization that provides research and policy analysis on both United States and foreign health systems. Also at the CHA site is the Project HOPE Walsh Center for Rural Health Affairs, which conducts research on issues affecting health care in rural America. Also on this site is the journal *Health Affairs*.

Public Broadcasting Service
http://www.pbs.org

This site is searchable and has information relating to programs produced by PBS. For those checking out the future of the world wide web, this is a good place to see it in action—assuming your computer software communications package can support the bells and whistles! One of the more fascinating parts of this site, and one that is useful to nonprofit executives, is a section that provides transcripts of the *Online NewsHour* (what used to be known as the *MacNeil-Lehrer Report* before Robin MacNeil retired) and RealAudio of the past week's programs. A search on the term "nonprofit" turned up more than thirty documents in the program's archives, none of the references more than two years old. The term "managed care," by contrast, yielded 2,228 documents (but that included duplicates, unfortunately). This is one of the best sites produced by broadcast media and, considering the in-depth nature of the programming, particularly its public policy offerings, one of the most valuable as well. If you are researching a public policy issue, it is worth the trip to this site to check out what's available. A site guide provides capsule summaries, in alphabetical order, of available content. The site also includes the

PBS Adult Learning Satellite Service. Using satellite delivery, this service offers resources for college courses, distance education, business training, and library media collections, all of which could be useful to your nonprofit.

This certificate series in nonprofit management is one of many courses offered through the PBS Adult Learning Satellite Service, available through the PBS web site.

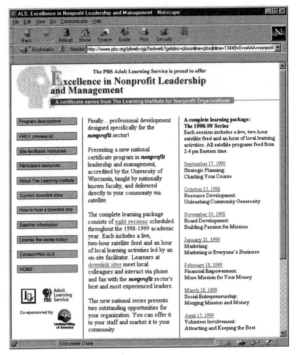

Used with permission.

Salvation Army

http://www.salvationarmy.org

The Salvation Army is an international humanitarian and social service organization administered by the evangelical part of the Universal Christian Church. The site's design is impressive—certainly not second-hand. This site has a clip art gallery in the Salvation Army Resources section with hundreds of pieces of downloadable clip art, including cartoons, that are in the public domain. Click on Resources, then Webmaster Resources, for practical advice and technical information about building a web site. The site is a good source of material for news relating to natural disasters—the Salvation Army is always on the scene. It includes the expected sectarian messages, but it is not offensive to those who do not share the religious fervor of the organization's members and leadership.

Second Harvest

http://www.secondharvest.org

Founded in 1979, Second Harvest is the largest domestic hunger relief organization in the United States, providing nearly a billion pounds of food each year to the needy. The site includes an events calendar and a secure form to make online donations. Visitors can send holiday cards with their handwritten name for a $10 donation. The legislative section under Issues and Events includes a biweekly electronic newsletter, *Legislative Harvest*, on issues of importance to food banks. There is good information concerning natural disasters. The Action Alerts explain each issue targeted for advocacy and include what actions are requested. Also on the site is the quarterly magazine *Second Harvest Update.* Click on Watchdog Report Card for links to organizations that monitor charities, and information about obtaining a hard copy of the organization's 990 tax return and annual report.

Shriners Hospital for Crippled Children

http://www.shrinershq.org

Shriners Hospitals for Children is a network of twenty-two pediatric specialty hospitals that provide free medical care for youngsters under eighteen years of age. The site includes excerpts from *Between Us* magazine, information about obtaining free health care for kids, donor information, and useful consumer information files. Among them are power mower safety tips, advice on burn prevention, and information on preventing birth defects.

UJA Federations of North America

http://www.uja.org

UJA Federations is a partnership of the Council of Jewish Federations, United Jewish Appeal, and United Israel Appeal to form the "efficient core of a continental system servicing hundreds of [Jewish] Federations and independent communities," according to the web site. The Council of Jewish Federations is the continental association of 189 Jewish federations, the local community fundraising and social service/education management organizations of the Jewish community. Included on the site is the North American Jewish Data Bank, which is a repository for computer-based population and survey data on Jewish communities in the United States

A chart from the UJA Federations of North America computer-based population data.

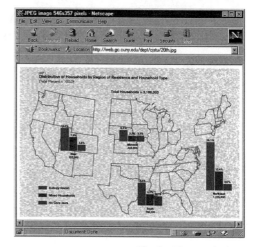

Used with permission.

and Canada. The Other Jewish Websites button is a link to hundreds of Jewish organizations around the world.

United Negro College Fund
http://www.uncf.org

The United Negro College Fund is an educational assistance organization with forty private, historically black, member colleges and universities. The first vision that hits the screen when this page loads is a box with "Pledge to College Fund/UNCF" inside it. Obviously, a potential donor is a terrible thing to waste. With a click or two, you are transported to an online pledge form. There are links to the organization's Frederick D. Patterson Research Institute and the UNCF/Merck Science Initiative. The institute has information and statistical data relating to African-American education. The home page is a pleasantly designed gateway to files about the organization's history, local affiliates, member institutions, programs, and scholarships.

United Way's site has many useful links for nonprofit managers and fundraisers.

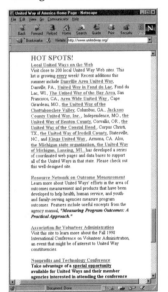

Used with permission.

United Way/Crusade of Mercy
http://www.unitedway.org

The United Way system includes nearly 1,400 community-based United Way organizations, each independent, separately incorporated, and governed by local volunteers. Through a single community-wide campaign, local United Way volunteers raise funds to support local agency service providers and provide funding to 45,000 agencies and chapters. The site has links to many pages of interest to people who manage or raise funds for nonprofits. There are links to a number of local United Ways, a list of web sites for people involved with public policy research, and many other resources. This site includes a resource network on outcome management and pages devoted to quality improvement (click on the Latest in Continuous Quality Improvement). There is also a nifty Y2K Technical Guide that can be downloaded in PDF format.

World Vision USA
http://www.worldvision.org

According to this web site, "World Vision is one of the world's largest child sponsorship organizations. During 1996, 1,164,410 children in 47 countries were sponsored by World Vision." The home page links viewers to files designated as Learn (About Us), Explore (The World), Know (The Facts), and Change (A Life). New material is posted periodically. The Know button links to pages relating to *World Hunger* magazine, press releases, commentary, statistics about the organization's work, and information about the famine in North Korea. The Explore button links to files about the organization's programs around the world and includes a three-day virtual expedition to Honduras conducted by four staff members. The Change button tells viewers how they can donate and volunteer, and there is an extensive frequently asked questions file on the site—a good example of how an international charity can communicate effectively with the public. Finally, the site includes a topical index, which is helpful for navigating it quickly.

YMCA of the USA
http://www.ymca.net

Collectively, local YMCAs make up the country's largest community service organization. Included on the site is a button for finding your local YMCA, which allows you to search by ZIP code or city and state for locations nearest you. Other buttons link you to information about YMCA programs, categorized by kids, families, and communities, and link you to *Discovery YMCA*, the quarterly magazine of the YMCA of the USA. There are also links to all local YMCAs with web sites. In the Families area, you can find tips on parenting, press releases, statements, and survey findings.

Others Charities of Interest

Alzheimer's Association
http://www.alz.org

There are five sections to this nicely designed, frame-supported site. The Facts contains answers to frequently asked questions about the disease and a file of facts and figures. Taking Care provides information about living with the disease and other caregiver issues. Medical Issues provides files about diagnosis and treatment. Research is the gateway to files research, grants, and the Reagan Institute. About Us details the organization's mission, vision, goals, annual report, conferences, and advocacy activity.

America's Charities
http://www.charities.org

America's Charities, established in 1980, is a nonprofit federation of more than one hundred national charities. In addition to links to the pages of its members, there is a link to individuals who coordinate volunteers for its membership by region. The pitch made by the organization is to purchase its services to set up payroll deduction workplace campaigns and provide the fiscal management for funneling the collections to worthy charities. And guess who's on the list of these worthy charities? Its members, of course!

Charity Village
http://www.charityvillage.com

Various categories of information available on Charity Village's site.

Used with permission.

This is a bilingual site (French and English) serving Canadian charities, but it is certainly of interest to those of us down south as well. There's news about the latest developments, pages for both nonprofit managers and those who donate, a career center, book reviews, and lots of useful files and links. The intent here is similar to the one-stop shopping you find at the Internet Non-Profit Center. It is colorful, inviting, and updated daily. The Virtual Village is divided into sections designated NewsWeek, the Career Centre, the Bus Station, the Library, Downtown, the Park, and the Town Hall. The Bus Station, for example, has links to online resources. The site consists of more than two thousand pages and is a cornucopia of valuable nonprofit organization information.

Independent Charities of America
http://www.independentcharities.org

Independent Charities of America (ICA) was founded in 1988 by a group of volunteer employee-givers to serve employees who donate to charities, to provide a cost-effective alternative to company support of employee giving at work, and to provide one-stop application, certification, and access to workplace and other federated fundraising for charities who agree to abide by the standards of ICA. The site helps web surfers find charities that meet their interests and includes links to those charities. The site also can help you track down public speakers from its member charities; you send them an e-mail for more information. The database is searchable and has a secure, online form for donations.

Make-A-Wish Foundation

http://www.wish.org

The mission of the organization is to grant the wishes of children with terminal or life-threatening illnesses. The frames-based site opened with the option to open a video clip of Make-A-Wish granting its 50,000th wish. Buttons include links to files headlined Make-A-Wish Story, Chapter Listing, What Is Make-A-Wish?, How Are Wishes Granted?, How To Donate, Chain Letter Information (relating to an unauthorized internet chain letter encouraging people to send business cards to a seriously ill boy), Potpourri of Wishes, Frequently Asked Questions, Guest Book, Our National Speakers Bureau, Major Make-A-Wish Sponsors, and News Center (organizational press releases).

Prospect Research Sites

Following are a few sites useful to fundraisers involved in prospect research. A search through the links on these sites and the use of internet search engines will help you uncover more sites.

The Association of Prospect Researchers for Advancement

http://Weber.u.washington.edu/~dlamb/apra/APRA.html

The Association of Prospect Researchers for Advancement (APRA) fosters professional growth for development researchers. This site provides a place where new and experienced prospect research professionals can learn about prospect research, the professional organization, its events, and services. It features a job posting section, a publication available for download, and other information useful to fundraisers involved in prospect research.

Hoover's Online

http://hoovWeb.hoovers.com

Hoover's Online has extensive, detailed, and well-organized information on more than 3,400 public and private companies. This subscription service offers much for free, including 13,000 company "capsules" (shorter information pages) that may be sufficient for many fundraising uses. Searches can be performed by company name, ticker symbol, keywords, or a company officer's name. Members have access to full company profiles and more powerful research capabilities. For the investor, Hoovers Online offers this and much more, but for the prospect researcher it can also be most valuable.

Internet Prospector

http://w3.uwyo.edu/~prospect

This site features a free monthly online newsletter directed to nonprofit fundraisers. Information on this site is gleaned by volunteers who "mine" the internet for fundraising nuggets, and the site is organized as a collaborative effort of fundraising colleagues. For those who may forget to check in on a regular basis, there is a subscription form for issues sent via e-mail. Past newsletters are archived at the site. Each newsletter focuses on sites of interest to fundraisers and prospect researchers. It is organized into categories, such as corporations, foundations/grants, people, ethics, news online, international, tools, and access (prospect research pages). This site is a wonderful starting point for finding many other resources related to prospect research or for brainstorming on new prospects. It is also to be applauded as one of the more friendly sites (for example, reproduction of the material with copyrights is encouraged) and for its success as a team effort among individuals helping one another to enhance philanthropy for all.

Internet Prospector's archives page.

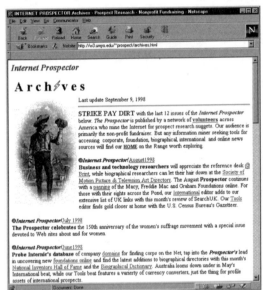

Used with permission.

The Informant

http://informant.dartmouth.edu

This unique and free service is an excellent tool for doing prospect research while you sleep. It saves your favorite search engine queries and web sites, checks them periodically, and sends you e-mail notification when there are new or updated web pages. You can enter up to three sets of keywords. At regular intervals, the Informant uses several popular search engines to find ten web pages that are most relevant to your keywords. The Informant will also watch five of your favorite web pages and will e-mail you when they are updated. Though the service is free, you must register as a user and log in with a password, which protects people who are doing searches that are personal in nature, such as health concerns.

David Lamb's Prospect Research Page
http://Weber.u.washington.edu/~dlamb/research.html

This is a handy list of prospect research sites run by David Lamb, director of donor acknowledgments and prospect research at the University of Washington in Seattle. The site is organized according to what you are researching: corporations and executives, professionals, foundations, news sources, and more. David Lamb has done a very good job of keeping this site focused on links of real value to prospect researchers.

PR Newswire
http://www.prnewswire.com

PR Newswire presents current press releases from companies, foundations, and other organizations. If you need to know when your prospect's company is sold or how their lawsuit is doing, then this may be a helpful place to start.

Donor Assistance Sites

Council of Better Business Bureaus
(see pages 10–11 for description)
http://www.bbb.org

International Service Agencies (ISA)
(see page 11 for description)
http://www.charity.org

National Charities Information Bureau
http://www.give.org

This site is aimed at donors who wish to ensure that they are giving to charitable organizations that fit this organization's guidelines. Interested donors can order the organization's *Wise Giving Guide* at no cost. By signing on, donors will receive notification via e-mail of new information made available at the site. There is also a set of donor tips available at the site. An online reference guide can be used by donors to review whether any of three hundred organizations evaluated comply with the standards of the National Charities Information Bureau. These standards are detailed at the site and relate to the organization's governance, purpose, and its programs. They also cover information disclosure, methods of fundraising, reporting, budgeting, and the use of funds, among other criteria. The quick reference guide provides an easily scanned alphabetical list of organizations coded as to whether they adhere to the recommended standards and whether information has not been disclosed by the organization. Every week, a new charity is featured, with the results of its report published.

The Non-Profit Internet Handbook

Did you know that this publication is an excerpt from *The Non-Profit Internet Handbook*, published in 1998 by White Hat Communications? *The Non-Profit Internet Handbook* is the definitive handbook for non-profit organizations that want to get the most out of the internet. This is a valuable resource for

- Non-profit organization executive staff
- Non-profit organization board members
- Those who fund non-profit organizations
- Those who contribute time and money to non-profit organizations

The Non-Profit Internet Handbook includes:

- How to connect to the internet
- How to do effective fund-raising and advocacy on the internet
- How to develop your organization's world wide web site
- How to find information useful to non-profits on the internet
- How to locate online sources of government foundation and private corporation grants

Plus: Reviews of more than 250 of the most valuable internet sites for non-profit organizations! This book is illustrated with internet-related cartoons drawn by the internationally acclaimed cartoonist Randy Glasbergen, creator of *The Better Half*.

The Non-Profit Internet Handbook is an essential reference publication for every non-profit executive's bookshelf.

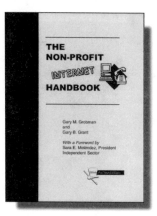

ISBN 0-9653653-6-0
8½" x 11" softcover
216 pages plus index

Published by White Hat Communications

"If you want to understand the internet, with all that it has to offer — if you want to know exactly how the internet can be useful to your non-profit, how it can increase your interaction with your constituency and serve to spread the word about your organization — if you need to learn to search the web for reliable, up-to-date information on what is happening in the non-profit world, and the world in general — The Non-Profit Internet Handbook is the perfect gateway to the internet galaxy."

— Sara E. Mélendez, president, Independent Sector

Collaboration Handbook:
Creating, Sustaining, and Enjoying the Journey
by Michael Winer and Karen Ray

Shows you how to get a collaboration going, define the results you're after, determine everyone's roles, create an action plan, and evaluate the results. Includes a case study of one collaboration from start to finish, helpful tips on how to avoid pitfalls, and worksheets to keep everyone on track.

192 pages, softcover   Item# AWF-94-CHC $30.00

Collaboration: What Makes It Work
by Wilder Research Center

An in-depth review of current collaboration research. Major findings are summarized, critical conclusions are drawn, and nineteen key factors influencing successful collaborations are identified. See if your collaboration's plans include the necessary ingredients.

53 pages, softcover   Item# AWF-92-CWW $15.00

Community Building: What Makes It Work
by Wilder Research Center

Shows you what really does (and doesn't) contribute to community building success. Reveals twenty-eight keys to help you build community more effectively. Includes detailed descriptions of each factor, case examples of how they play out, and practical questions to assess your own work.

112 pages, softcover   AWF-97-CWB $20.00

Consulting with Nonprofits:
A Practitioner's Guide
by Carol A. Lukas

A step-by-step, comprehensive guide for consultants working with nonprofit and community organizations. Addresses the art of consulting, how to run your business, and much more. Also includes tips and anecdotes from thirty skilled consultants.

240 pages, softcover   AWF-98-CWN $35.00

Coping with Cutbacks: The Nonprofit Guide to Success When Times Are Tight
by Emil Angelica and Vincent Hyman

Devolution—the delegation of power from the federal government to local governments—means BIG changes for nonprofits, including far less government funding. This guide provides a process for finding creative ways to meet your mission goals by expanding and deepening your nonprofit's connection to the community. Also includes 180 cutback strategies you can put to use right away. Your organization doesn't have to be in a financial crisis in order to benefit from this book.

128 pages, softcover   AWF-97-CWC $20.00

Marketing Workbook for Nonprofit Organizations Volume I: Develop the Plan
by Gary J. Stern

Don't just wish for results—get them! Here's how to create a straightforward, usable marketing plan. Includes the six P's of Marketing, how to use them effectively, a sample marketing plan, and detachable worksheets.

132 pages, softcover   AWF-90-MW1 $28.00

Marketing Workbook for Nonprofit Organizations Volume II:
Mobilize People for Marketing Success
by Gary J. Stern

Put together a successful promotional campaign based on the most persuasive tool of all: personal contact. Learn how to mobilize your entire organization, its staff, volunteers, and supporters in a focused, one-to-one marketing campaign. Provides step-by-step instructions, sample agendas for motivational trainings, and worksheets to keep the campaign organized and on track. Also includes *Pocket Guide for Marketing Representatives*. In it, your marketing representatives can record key campaign messages and find motivational reminders.

192 pages, softcover   AWF-97-MW2 $28.00

Resolving Conflict in Nonprofit Organizations: The Leader's Guide to Finding Constructive Solutions

by Marion Peters Angelica

Helps you identify conflict, decide whether to intervene, and shows you how to plan and carry out a conflict resolution process. Includes exercises to learn and practice conflict resolution skills, guidance on handling unique conflicts such as harassment and discrimination, and when (and where) to seek outside help with litigation, arbitration, and mediation.

192 pages, softcover   Item# AWF-99-RCN $28.00

Strategic Planning Workbook for Nonprofit Organizations, Revised and Updated

by Bryan Barry

Chart a wise course for your nonprofit's future. This time-tested workbook gives you practical step-by-step guidance, real-life examples, one nonprofit's complete strategic plan, and easy-to-use worksheets.

144 pages, softcover   Item# AWF-97-SPW $28.00

The Wilder Nonprofit Field Guide Series

Dive right in with these shorter books on specific topics

The Wilder Nonprofit Field Guide to: Conducting Successful Focus Groups

by Judith Sharken Simon

Shows how to collect valuable information without a lot of money or special expertise. Using this proven technique, you'll get essential opinions and feedback to help you check out your assumptions, do better strategic planning, improve services or products, build goodwill, and more.

$15.00   80 pages, softcover   Item# AWF-99-FGC

The Wilder Nonprofit Field Guide to: Developing Effective Teams

by Beth Gilbertsen and Vijit Ramchandani

Helps you understand, start, and maintain a team. Provides tools and techniques for writing a mission statement, setting goals, conducting effective meetings, creating ground rules to manage team dynamics, making decisions in teams, creating project plans, and developing team spirit.

80 pages, softcover   Item# AWF-99-FGD $15.00

The Wilder Nonprofit Field Guide to: Getting Started on the Internet

by Gary M. Grobman & Gary B. Grant

Learn how to use the internet for everything from finding job candidates to finding solutions to management problems. Includes a list of useful nonprofit sites, and shows you how to use the internet to uncover valuable information and help your nonprofit be more productive.

64 pages, softcover   Item# AWF-99-FGG $15.00

Violence Prevention and Intervention Books

The Wilder Publishing Center also publishes books on violence prevention and intervention. To get a FREE catalog with more information, please call **1-800-274-6024.** Details on all our publications are also available on our web site at **www.wilder.org.** Here are the titles of our current books:

The Little Book of Peace

Journey Beyond Abuse: A Step-by-Step Guide to Facilitating Women's Domestic Abuse Groups

Moving Beyond Abuse *(participant's workbook to Journey Beyond Abuse)*

Foundations for Violence-Free Living: A Step-by-Step Guide to Facilitating Men's Domestic Abuse Groups

On the Level *(participant's workbook to Foundations for Violence-Free Living)*

What Works in Preventing Rural Violence

Five EasyWays to Order

 Call toll-free: 1-800-274-6024
Internationally: 651-659-6024

Fax: 651-642-2061

E-mail: books@wilder.org
On-line: www.wilder.org

Mail: Amherst H. Wilder Foundation
Publishing Center
919 Lafond Avenue
St. Paul, MN 55104

Sales tax

Minnesota residents, please add 7% sales tax or attach your tax exempt certificate. FED TAX ID 41-0693889

Shipping & Handling (to each delivery address)

If order totals:	Ground 7-10 business days	Priority 2-3 business days	Next Day Next day by 5:00 pm
Up to $30.00	$4.00	$6.00	$35.00
$30.01 - 60.00	$5.00	$7.00	$40.00
$60.01 - 150.00	$6.00	$8.00	$45.00
$150.01 - 500.00	$8.00	$10.00	$50.00
Over $500.00	3% of order	Call	Call

Priority and Next Day Air orders called or faxed in by 2:00 p.m. EST M-F will be shipped the same day. **Priority and Next Day orders must be prepaid. Outside the U.S. or Canada, add an additional U.S. $5.00.**

Quantity discounts

We offer substantial discounts on orders of ten or more copies of any single title. Please call for details.

www.wilder.org

Want more details? Check out our web site for each book's table of contents, author information, excerpts, and discounts. You can also order on-line.

Order Form   Prices subject to change

	ITEM #	QTY.	PRICE EACH	TOTAL AMOUNT
Collaboration Handbook	AWF-94-CHC		$30.00	
Collaboration: What Makes It Work	AWF-92-CWW		15.00	
Community Building: What Makes It Work	AWF-97-CBW		20.00	
Consulting with Nonprofits	AWF-98-CWN		35.00	
Coping with Cutbacks	AWF-97-CWC		20.00	
Marketing Workbook Volume I: Develop the Plan	AWF-90-MW1		28.00	
Marketing Workbook Volume II: Mobilize People	AWF-97-MW2		28.00	
Resolving Conflict in Nonprofit Organizations	AWF-99-RCN		28.00	
Strategic Planning Workbook	AWF-97-SPW		28.00	
Wilder Field Guide: Conducting Successful Focus Groups	AWF-99-FGC		15.00	
Wilder Field Guide: Developing Effective Teams	AWF-99-FGD		15.00	
Wilder Field Guide: Fundraising on the Internet	AWF-99-FGF		15.00	
Wilder Field Guide: Getting Started on the Internet	AWF-99-FGG		15.00	

Send to (please print or attach business card)

Name _____

Organization _____

Address _____

_____

City _____ State _____ ZIP _____

Phone *(in case we have questions)* (_____) _____

We occasionally make our mailing list available to carefully selected companies. If you do not wish to have your name included, please check here ☐

VISA MasterCard AMERICAN EXPRESS **Cards**

Payment Method

Card # _____

Expiration Date _____

Signature (required) _____

☐ Check/Money Order (payable to A. H. Wilder Foundation)

☐ Bill Me (for orders under $100) PO # _____

SUBTOTAL	
7% tax if in MN	
SHIPPING	
TOTAL	

We'd like to hear your comments! Please fill out the short survey on other side ☞

Customer Feedback Survey

Dear Reader,

Please take a few moments to give us your feedback. Your responses will help us improve future editions of this book, and will help us improve our service to you. You can either mail the survey to Wilder Publishing Center, 919 Lafond Avenue, St. Paul, MN, USA 55104 or fax it to 651-642-2061. Thank you for your time!

How would you rate this book with regard to its:	Terrible	Poor	OK	Good	Very Good	Out-standing
1. Fit with what you were looking for						
2. Usefulness compared to other materials you've looked at in the same general topic area						
3. Usefulness as a stand alone resource—without the help of a consultant						
4. Organization of information						
5. Overall appearance						
6. Price compared to other books you use in your profession						
7. Amount of time it took to receive your order						
8. Quality of customer service						
9. Condition of the book when it arrived						

10. What is your overall impression of books from the Wilder Foundation?

11. Have you done anything new or different as a result of the information in this publication? If so, what? If not, why not?

12. Is the process outlined in this book easy to follow, or could it be improved?

13. Where do you normally buy or look for books on topics of interest to nonprofit organizations?

14. Do you have any suggestions for books we should develop that would help you in your work?

15. Any other comments?

Your title and organization (optional): _____

THANK YOU! Your comments will help us improve the quality of our publications.